Read*ux*

Readux Books: Series 1, № 4

Copyright © 2013 by Gideon Lewis-Kraus
All rights reserved

ISBN: 978-3-944801-03-2

Cover illustration by André Gottschalk
Design by Susann Stefanizen

Published by Readux Books
Sorauer Str. 16, 10997 Berlin, Germany

www.readux.net

City of Rumor:
The Compulsion to Write About Berlin

Gideon Lewis-Kraus

There is a measure of unaccountable time you can spend in Berlin and write it off as extended-holiday frippery. But there comes a Rubiconic moment, after which you'll find it hard to leave without having something to say for yourself. You've probably gone to Berlin in part because of its reputation for world-historical fun. If you've found yourself there in some bounded way—on a fellowship before graduate school, say— the fun serves just fine. But if your move is an open-ended affair, the fun takes its course, and then, to avoid that obscure sense of having failed at being somewhere, you need an exit strategy. Some exit strategies allow you to stay: falling in love with a German, say, or going to German graduate school. Other exit visas allow you to leave. Falling in love with someone in Paris. Getting a job in London. You need some finding that retroactively validates the whole experiment. Because you've set yourself up, is the thing. As a writer, I hoped I might find that justification in telling a story that looped the whole thing together in a reasonable way. For a time I thought I'd accomplished that—I wrote a book that began with a story about how I ended up in Berlin, what I did and, more importantly, did not do there, and why and how I managed to leave—and I looked forward to never having to write about Berlin again. I have found, however, that I cannot shake the urge to write more about Berlin, to revise what I have already written about Berlin, and furthermore to disclaim in advance as insufficiently definitive anything I might conceivably write about Berlin in the future. I am tempted now to say that this in and of itself reveals something definitive about Berlin, something about the impossibility of saying anything definitive about Berlin. The infinite regressions of the place remain with you long after you've left. They remain with you even after you've quit writing that you've quit writing about the why and what of it all.

When I decided to move to Berlin it was at least in part because it seemed like the sort of place where one might plausibly become a writer. San Francisco, where I'd been living for no reason, seemed to me the sort of place one might write book reviews, which is what I'd been doing. In Berlin, in contrast, whatever I paid attention to would be something necessarily novel, which meant that the writing I'd go on to produce about such novelties would justify the fact that I had somewhat sheepishly taken to calling myself a writer. The plan, though, had never been to write about Berlin, exactly. This is strange, I realize now. I wonder what it was that I did plan to write, if I wasn't going to write a novel and I wasn't going to write about what it was like to live in this novel-seeming place.

Furthermore, my interest in the work of famous expatriate writers had never really been in the novels they'd incidentally produced while living in novel places. It was in their subsequent accounts, for which their novels had produced an appetite and an audience, of the conditions under which their novels were written. I had no particular use for *The Sun Also Rises*, but I really liked *A Moveable Feast*. *The Berlin Stories*, with which most incoming Anglophones were summarily outfitted, was fine, but I vastly preferred Isherwood's journals. What I liked most, it turned out, was reading about the time in which these writers weren't writing. All of which is to say it ought to have come as no surprise that I got very little writing done there, at least during my initial tenures.

This is not strictly true. I did do writing. I wrote about some Jewish goings-on for a magazine that, like many New York publications, had numberless berths for Holocaust-related items. I also wrote a story for a New York magazine about the New York publishing world, on the occasion of their annual trip to the Frankfurt Book Fair, but only because that magazine was, and remains, cost-conscious, and it was cheaper for me to take the train than for them to fly someone over, and because they'd already asked twenty-seven other people, all of whom had thought it a foolish thing to agree to do. I wrote a little bit about art, because art was one of the things putatively going on in novel Berlin, but I never intended to be an art writer.

So the first real writing I did—or, rather, the first writing I did that was meaningful to me, and at my own devising—after I moved to Berlin came long after I'd lost any illusions about what it might be like to live there, or rather the kind of writer I might become there. It was, in fact, a piece of writing motivated and framed by the decision to be anywhere but Berlin—or, more specifically, to be in the sustained incremental process of moving away from Berlin. I walked the Camino de Santiago—a medieval Catholic pilgrimage across northern Spain that has become popular with a young, secular, international crowd—at least in part on a lark, but the substance of the lark was that Berlin had come to represent a place where nobody got up in the morning, and when they did get up it was with some reservations about the prospect of the day, whereas on the Camino everybody woke up at five in the morning and, without further ado, began to walk west. Formally, it was the opposite of Berlin.

Which is how, years after having moved to Berlin to become a writer, a city which I'd never intended to write about itself—if I had, I'd have taken better notes, though at least I had long emails home—I ended up trying to describe the nature of the free-for-all that had both led me to and away from that city. The proximate reason for this account was the book I ended up writing, about pilgrimage. The essay about Berlin, however, never quite agreed with the rest of the book. This was to some extent by design. My life in Berlin, with its pointedly free-floating anxiety, provided a stark contrast to the anchored, pointless equanimity I felt while en route to some distant, arbitrary elsewhere.

The chapters of the book that were not about Berlin are of little interest to us here except insofar as they took up the idea of freedom via constraint, where Berlin, at least the Berlin of auspicious rumor, was all about freedom from constraint. This counterpoint structured the way I came to tell the story. The chapters about pilgrimage, like the pilgrimages themselves, were rather neatly constrained by their narrative necessity: I began in one place, ended in another, and the eventfulness in between was in order. They were easy stories to tell.

The chapter about Berlin, like the lives of many of the people I knew in Berlin, had no such constraint—no relevant chronology, no narrative necessity. When I sat down to write about Berlin for the first time, all I could do was make a list of anecdotes, the ones that had lingered with me for some reason, in no particular order. I wrote them out as a series of disordered episodes—the time we followed the votive candles to the rave in the toolshed in the middle of the park, the time our friend held a real art opening outside a fake art opening—and saw little use or accuracy in connecting them. After all, they had only ever felt associatively connected in the first place. They had, of course, happened in one particular order, though as far as I could tell they might very well have happened in any other order, or no order at all.

I revised those anecdotes more compulsively than I did any other section of the book, and, more than any other section of the book, they changed with each revision. I cannot look at them now without feeling inadequate, if not fraudulent: embarrassed and disappointed by the essay's omissions and mischaracterizations. I can't return to Berlin without wishing I'd written something entirely different. But each time I return, I find that what I wish I'd written has once again changed.

*

When I first wrote out the series of anecdotes that became my Berlin chapter, I was leaving for what I then was sure was the last time, having, to my mind, achieved very little there. It was, after all, only in leaving Berlin that I'd felt inspired to write, and what I'd felt inspired to write about was why walking arbitrarily west in the Spanish heat for a month felt vastly more productive than my life in Berlin ever had. My bitterness had an admonitory quality. Had you asked me at the time whom I was writing about Berlin for, I think I might have said— or, in any case, ought to have said—that I was writing it for other people who had moved to Berlin without having enough insight to realize what was going on there, or for that matter wasn't going on, how little it had to do with what they'd gone there to do, how little it had to do with anything at all, and that, frankly, they really ought to leave. I was basically congratulating myself on having at last understood that the jig was up.

That the jig had in fact never been all that operative to begin with. The first stab at those anecdotes, finished in my brother's serviced apartment in Shanghai—a place, it seemed to me, where people expatriated themselves to get things done—was thus written with what I thought of as clear-eyed disillusionment. I was very pleased with my ability to describe our voids. With no real work to speak of, love, or at least sex, took on unreasonable burdens. Structured productive time was creatively supplanted by structured consumptive time. We repressively desublimated. In the absence of actual poetry, we took very seriously the receding prospect of becoming the poets of our own lives. This was the tenor of the material I cut:

> *The rest of us hung around at the openings in the spaces and tried to look good and smoked. There was a lot of smoking to do all the time; I didn't even like cigarettes, had never liked cigarettes, but at a certain point, the minute I arrived at Tegel airport, I had to accept the fact that the great storehouses of cigarettes in Berlin weren't going to smoke themselves. The cigarettes marked off the time: when you finished one, it was time to light another one. In this way the moments arrayed themselves in an order. They gave you something to focus on, for a few minutes, anyway.*

Sex did this, too. There was some pretense of sexual adventure but it was mostly just unaccountability. We were not careful with each other's feelings, or with our own. We acknowledged that Berlin was part audition in recklessness. This could feel both exhilarating and very painful, depending on how unflappable we could be. What was so awful more or less half the time wasn't so much feeling sad or anxious as it was feeling ashamed to be sad or anxious; it felt as though I was reneging on my commitment to emancipation, and squandering this exercise in freedom. There were times it got very bad. Shortly before one dawn or another someone looked across my kitchen table at me and said, through the suspended hours of smoke, "Look, life is long and you sleep with a lot of people." Whether it was supposed to be an explanation or a consolation I am still unsure. What I remember of the moment is that I was afraid that if I allowed myself to tear she would find me even less interesting than I worried she already did.

It was, of course, easy to joke about all of this. A gay friend, a few months after he'd arrived, complained that his group of friends had developed an orgy habit. He was young and suspected this might be a homosexual problem. A friend, the sort of dazzling and unpredictable woman I'd come to Berlin to meet on her own terms, consoled him from the perspective of the straight minority. "You gays just sleep with everybody all at once," she said, "whereas we have just chosen to do it one by one." She didn't say this just for our friend's benefit. What she said was true and heartbreaking.

When you did very little with your days there was great pressure to compensate in the evenings, which is why evenings so often relaxed dementedly into mornings. In Berlin we witnessed dawn with nontrivial regularity. This schedule solved, with some success, the problem of what to do with the daytime. It made it go away. Shortly after the orgy crisis, our young gay friend got a job, in a gallery. He sat in front of an iMac the size of a drive-in theater, received real-time updates from his friends in New York, and was paid to be contemptuous of visitors. We were falling-down drunk at the former city bath one night and I asked him how the job was going. "It's great," he said. "Now I have something to do besides sit around all day and wait for it to be"—he looked at his watch— "eight p.m."

For a time it was important to me that this writing about Berlin appear on its own, outside the context of the book, because it felt to me like more than just introductory material. I sent to it an editor I had long admired. He wrote back that he liked the piece a lot, would be glad to publish it, but that he thought I needed one more revision. "Your contempt for the various figures you describe is clear towards the end of the piece, but it has to be present throughout. No radical changes are required, but readers will naturally be so disgusted by this parade of Ivy League privilege and fake-rebel aristos that you have to signal somehow that you're on their side, in some world-weary way. Be thinking of Hemingway's descriptions of the artists in Paris."

His insistence that I harden my cynicism only made me realize the extent to which I had to ease it, and in the book almost the entirety of that section was ultimately cut, or rather radically refashioned.

In a way, the editor was right: the version I'd sent him was indeed saturated with contempt for the floating island of privilege I'd finally rescued myself from. After all, I was writing this in a year of global economic catastrophe—I moved to Berlin in the last year of a rising housing market, after years of attending antiwar demonstrations in San Francisco that felt more like picnics than protests, and stayed through two years of debates about TARP—and I wanted my accounting of the events to reflect the smug isolation of the time.

What I felt I was saying, then, was that most of us there had left during the boom and had thus freed ourselves from having to care about the bust. Two banker friends of friends happened to be in town during the Lehman meltdown. They stopped obsessively to check their BlackBerries, and we looked at our old Nokias and imagined that the events they were describing were happening in an alternate universe—a pretty fucked-up one, we might have added, on our way to get another €0.79 beer. One that we were glad to have borne no responsibility for. We felt that, just because we weren't necessarily economically privileged—most of us, in those days, supported ourselves, on five or eight thousand dollars a year—we weren't privileged at all. But at the same time, the editor's suggestion that I make my feelings of contempt more explicit made me reconsider whether contempt was precisely the right tone for this definitive thing about Berlin.

*

I did not turn back to those anecdotes for some six months. In the meantime, I walked a circuit of eighty-eight Buddhist temples on a rural Japanese island, returned to Shanghai for the great letdown of the World's Fair, and then left China for San Francisco, where I slept on a friend's couch and spent most of a summer working on my book. When I returned to the Berlin anecdotes, their tone felt utterly foreign to me. My time back in San Francisco—where I once again fell into the pleasant, over-sated routines that characterized my life before I moved to Berlin—made me long for the near-constant companionship and eventful unpredictability of my life in Berlin.

Now I looked back on that roseate expanse of unoccupied and unoccupiable hours with nostalgia. The art world, absent the real money that drove similar scenes in wealthier places, no longer seemed vain and pretentious; it was well-intentioned and experimental and excusably callow. The expatriate community wasn't wasting its days in cafes full of mismatched chairs and its nights in barely converted industrial hubs, it was taking reasonable advantage of Berlin's cheapness to eschew the drudgery of inherited ambition. I decided I no longer felt contemptuous, and that the people I knew in Berlin had never been anything like "fake rebel aristos." They were just trying to abstract away the issues of economic necessity in order to accept more openly the problems of freedom. If the first version of the anecdotes had been written to take to task those who had chosen to move to Berlin, my second version was written to inspire rue in those who hadn't. A friend in New York read it and said it made him feel chastened, as though he'd really missed out on something important. I took some pleasure in this. My first version of the anecdotes had justified my decision to leave Berlin, but my second had reached further back to justify my decision to go in the first place. Now I returned and added scenes of fizzy experimental exhilaration.

What I'd wanted to suggest was that there might have been some time wasted, but that this was simply the cost of having such unusual amounts of time at our disposal. Not everything was going to pan out, and, more importantly, it would probably take a long time for us to understand what had and had not panned out. In the meantime we were doing our best. One could comfortably defer the necessary accounting, suspecting that there would inevitably be some future vantage from which this risk would appear profitable. Unfortunately, the longer you waited, the higher the stakes of the account.

At the end of the summer, after another few months of wandering in various deserts, I boarded a twenty-four-hour train from Kiev back to Berlin. I'd sworn I'd never go back, but here I was once more, this time with an actual project at hand: to finish the book that had, in no small part, been taken up as the project that might recoup whatever it was I'd gambled and possibly lost in Berlin. In those three autumn months, despite the kind of persistent sexual turmoil that seemed inevitable in Berlin, I was more productive than I'd been in the previous three years I'd spent on and off there. I got up early, I worked all day, I never went out. I felt great.

Or, rather, that was what I told myself later, for the purposes of the book, the epilogue of which took place back in that newly productive Berlin. I worked a lot, to be sure, but each time I finished a new draft of a chapter I called up Emilie, the little party mouse I'd written about, to inquire into opportunities for delinquency, she and I would go out, and forty-eight hours later I'd go home and resume work. I may have been productive, but I certainly wasn't happy. I often felt lonely and depressed, just the way I'd always felt lonely and depressed in Berlin.

But by then, given the shape of the book, those were things that no longer quite fit. I'd finally managed to settle on a narrative about the meaning of my time in Berlin, and that narrative had necessities of its own. Those anecdotes I'd endlessly refashioned had found a legible trajectory, one that wasn't all that far off from the old Isherwood story: I'd come to Berlin as an expectant naif and left a hard-headed realist. The arc of the book itself began with large, abstract questions about the nature of freedom and obligation and ended with small, intimate answers about the possibility of reconciliation and forgiveness. This wasn't sidestepping; it was the point: unanswerable universal questions (posed by the anxious naif) are almost always asked as a way of avoiding the great difficulty of the particular ones (those faced by the anxious realist). The book's coda thus had to take place in Berlin and had to be about the achievement of a focus and discipline that had, in my earlier interims in Berlin, eluded me. The moral of my return to Berlin was that I had at last put myself in a position to live in Berlin on my own terms (ambition, resolve) and not on the terms I'd construed as Berlin's (depravity, irresponsibility, indolence). So it was. In the book as it was published, I felt I had achieved a balanced impression of the possible risks and possible rewards of life in a certain place at a certain time.

*

There is no part of me that ever feels an urge to revisit the material in my three pilgrimage chapters. As far as I'm concerned, those narratives are settled, which is to say that they continue to seem largely accurate, presumably recognizable to the people with whom I shared the experiences. I see scenes I might have included or deleted, but I see no irreconcilable remainder. I feel as though I've done justice—and not only to myself, but to those who came before and those who followed.

But the first time I came back to Berlin as a visitor, less than a year after having left what passed for an actual life there behind, all I could see were the remainders. What I'd left out, what I'd misrepresented. My protean, anecdotal version of events there may have felt static and conflicted, nothing like the neat story I'd come to tell in the book, but I'd lost something in giving up that sketchy, makeshift approach to a sketchy, makeshift place. For I did not go to Berlin as a naif and I did not emerge from it a cynic. I did not begin in exhilaration and end in despond. There was no arc that moved from one state to another. There were just both states, always.

Still, it felt impossible to give up the story I'd put so much time and energy into. I felt as though my tale, as insufficient as it was, had nonetheless recovered for me the necessity of the time I had spent there. Despite my misgivings, I felt I had no choice but to continue to believe in the linearity I'd come to impose on those anecdotes. I felt the force of all of this when I noticed, upon returning to Berlin, that, impossibly, people were somehow still newly arriving there. They had only been in town a few weeks or six months and still they couldn't believe their luck, couldn't believe that a place offered so much freedom and possibility. Though even at the time I could recognize how ugly it was to feel this way, I felt some revulsion for their greenness. I told myself I knew the end of the story, I knew how it all turned out, and I knew it because it had come to be written that way. They still believed in a Berlin I had leveled, and I had to patronize them to preserve my own shaky place in that unbuilt city.

Those newcomers were continuing to write about Berlin, and of course I paid attention to their anecdotes and the morals they drew from them, because despite it all, I was still waiting to see how and if it had panned out. I hoped for and worried about the ramifications of alternate narratives. And the discourse about Berlin had, since the time I moved there, changed. The stories they told were no longer breathless. They were cautionary. There was a long thing in the *New York Times Magazine*, a memoir by an Australian who had come to Berlin to make music with his band. They had, predictably, made no music, having chosen instead to sleep during the daytime, and after some six months or a year the band had broken up and they had all beaten a hasty retreat, at least one of them in fear of the authorities. The writer had returned to Australia, gotten a girlfriend, or perhaps reunited with the girlfriend he'd left behind, and taken a responsible job. He was now writing a novel about his time in Berlin. The way it had come to pan out for him was in the public recognition of the fact that it had not, in fact, panned out for him. He had rendered his time there a success via the insight that it was a failure. It turned his experience in Berlin into a mere lesson, an episode.

Naturally I thought he hadn't gotten it. Yes, he had heard the Sirenic call of Berlin, and yes, he had, ultimately gotten out. But he hadn't understood that the real triumph wasn't in leaving, it was in staying and learning to survive on one's own terms. It was showing Berlin that freedom could be tamed, or redeemed. It was only then, according to my own idea of Berlin, one I'd come to think of as definitive, that one could safely leave. This is how I felt on my second trip back to Berlin as a visitor, and on my third. Sometime after that third trip, an extremely cold and depressing few days the first week of one December, I got back to New York to read yet another Berlin account, this one on a popular website that catered toward the sort of person who was always thinking about leaving New York for Berlin. It was written by a young Canadian named Thomas Rogers; he'd been in New York for years, always struggling with visa-renewal issues, until one day he quit his job and bought a ticket to the Berlin he'd heard so much about. He'd been there for two months. I thought, two months, yes, I know where this is going. This will be the exhilaration story.

But I hadn't known where it was going. It nodded to the exhilaration story, acknowledged that the Berlin of rumor, though slightly more expensive now, still more or less held, and that he was glad for the chance to indulge. But he shifted rather quickly into the second story, the story of excess and paralysis. Gee, I thought, this cycle has gotten short. In my day, it took a year for the shine to wear off. Now it happens in a month or two. Soon it will be simultaneous: one will arrive in delight and disenchantment. One will only have to spend a week in Berlin to assimilate its prospect and its danger. The experience would come prepackaged. And at that point you wouldn't have to wonder whether it had panned out.

You could take this prepackaged rue as one more sign that, as has always been said of Berlin, it's over, that whatever made it interesting has drawn to a close. At the end of my chapter about Berlin, I wrote about the idea of a place being over. I wrote that there is no such thing as a place being over; there is just the experience of being confounded by the persistence of you, that a place is over when you feel as though it has not occasioned the transformations it promised. Not when the streets are lined with identically weathered cafes, or when the rent has risen to the point that you actually have to do some work once in a while, but when the sense of vast possibility has collapsed into terror or resignation.

On my fourth trip back to Berlin, still waiting to see if I now felt as though it had all panned out, I met Thomas Rogers in a bar I'd always loved, a bar that had produced some of my more acute and implacable memories. It had been called Bellman, but when I emailed Thomas and asked if it was still open, he said yes, but that it had changed its name. Now it was called Feldman. Otherwise it was exactly the same: same phonograph in the window, same candles on the tables, same scarred, stripped concrete walls. As Thomas talked about his own experiences in Berlin, in which he felt as though he was struggling as a writer—though from what I could tell he'd been fantastically prolific—it seemed to me that perhaps the measure of a place's over-ness wasn't that the story about it had gone from one of possibility to one of frustration. What would make something over is when nobody was interested in telling, or hearing, the Berlin story at all. When people did not identify a particular place with either promise or despair, with the fantasy of youth or the fantasy of maturity. It's when—rather than trying to write something definitive, or accepting that nothing definitive can ever be written—we stop writing anything at all. When we cease to worry whether, in the end, it has all panned out.

ALSO AVAILABLE FROM
GIDEON LEWIS-KRAUS

"If David Foster Wallace had written *Eat, Pray, Love* . . . Digressively brilliant and seriously hilarious."
—Gary Shteyngart, author of *Super Sad True Love Story*

"A story that is both searching and purposeful, one that forces the reader, like the pilgrim, to value the journey as much as the destination."
—*The New Yorker*

AVAILABLE NOW WHEREVER BOOKS AND E-BOOKS ARE SOLD

slow travel berlin

BERLIN - THE SLOW WAY

In the same way that the Slow Food revolution has created a compelling antithesis to the burgeoning Fast Food business, Slow Travel encourages people to resist "Fast" Travel – the frustratingly frequent habit of speeding through all the best known landmarks of a city in 24 or 48 hours – then leaving again. Slow Travel encourages us to slacken our pace, re-consider our motivations (and itineraries) and embrace a "less is more" instead of a "fast is better" ethos. It emboldens us to take pause. To think. To saunter instead of rush and enjoy the details instead of blurring past them.

We aim to facilitate any quest to get beneath the skin of the city a little, or discover it at a more leisurely pace. We offer an insider's view that will doubtless overlap from time to time with other Berlin travel sites, but will ultimately provide a unique and above all reliable resource that gives a broader, deeper perspective. We love this city and we want you to love it too.

www.slowtravelberlin.com

Gideon Lewis-Kraus

Gideon Lewis-Kraus has written about books and culture for publications such as *Wired*, *Harper's*, *GQ*, the *London Review of Books*, *The New York Times Magazine*, *n+1*, and *McSweeney's*. His digressive travel memoir, *A Sense of Direction*, about pilgrimage and restlessness, appeared this past spring from Riverhead Books.